CITIES OF THE WORLD

TOKYO

BY DEBORAH KENT

CHILDREN'S PRESS®
A Division of Scholastic Inc.
New York Toronto London Auckland Sydney
Mexico City New Delhi Hong Kong
Danbury, Connecticut

CONSULTANT

Kiyomi Kagawa
Lecturer and Coordinator
Japanese Program of African & Asian Languages
Northwestern University

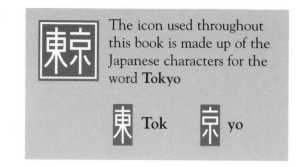

The icon used throughout this book is made up of the Japanese characters for the word **Tokyo**

東 Tok 京 yo

Project Editor: Downing Publishing Services
Design Director: Karen Kohn & Associates
Photo Researcher: Jan Izzo
Pronunciations: Courtesy of Tony Breed, M.A., Linguistics, University of Chicago

---

NOTES ON JAPANESE PRONUNCIATION

In Japanese, there is no stress. All syllables should be pronounced with equal stress. It sounds a little as if each syllable is a word. The English sentence "You go, too" sounds very much like a Japanese word. Sometimes, *n*, *m*, or *ng* is a whole syllable in Japanese. It should be spoken as if it were a regular syllable. If you say the word "button" quickly, the "n" sound at the end is like the Japanese *n* syllable. In this book, those syllables are written NN, MM, or NG. In Japanese, there is no difference between *r* and *l*. There is only one sound. It is usually written *r*, but it actually sounds more like *l*. Here, we have used *r*, except in the case of *ry*, for which we used *ly*. In some words, a syllable is not completely pronounced. It is whispered. We have written these in small capital letters. Finally, in Japanese there are long and short vowels and long and short consonants. Each long vowel is spoken about twice the length of time as a short vowel. In those cases, we have written it twice: DOH-OH, for instance. The vowels in Japanese are AH as in hot; EE as in heat; OO as in cook; EH as in bet; and OH as in boat.

LIBRARY OF CONGRESS CATALOGING-IN-PUBLICATION DATA

Kent, Deborah.
    Tokyo / by Deborah Kent
      p. cm. — (Cities of the world)
    Includes index.
    Summary: Describes Japan's capital city including its subway system, its streets and buildings, its celebrations of ancient religious traditions, and its sports and theater.
    ISBN 0-516-00354-2
    1. Tokyo (Japan)—Juvenile literature. [1. Tokyo (Japan)]
I. Title. II. Series: Cities of the world (New York, N.Y.)
DS896.35.K46 1996   95-39242
952' . 135—dc20   CIP
          AC

TABLE OF CONTENTS

EMPEROR

Every evening, flocks of wild birds stream above the streets of downtown Tokyo. Beyond the glass-and-steel office buildings, the birds have an ancient refuge. They sail over moats and walls into the peaceful forest on the grounds of the Imperial Palace.

The forest stands on the hills of central Tokyo. The tops of its trees nod gently over massive stone walls. Joggers pound along the path surrounding the outer moat. The palace grounds cover 264 acres. They are closed to the public for most of the year. The area is a private oasis of gardens, woods, and ponds. The emperor's estate preserves a bit of nature in the very heart of the busy city.

The ancient Japanese art of flower arrranging is still practiced today.

The palace is home to Japan's imperial family. It has been built and rebuilt many times over the centuries. Today's emperor lives in modern quarters with all the latest conveniences. Nearby lies the ruined stone foundation of Edo Castle.

Japanese children feeding Tokyo's pigeons

A view of the Imperial Gardens on the grounds of the Imperial Palace

The castle's 200-foot tower watched over the city nearly 500 years ago.

Japan is one of the most modern nations in the world. Tokyo is its bustling capital. The city is a tribute to modern architecture and engineering. It is also plagued with pollution, overcrowding, and all the other problems that go hand in hand with industry and development.

Tokyo deeply honors its past. It celebrates ancient religious traditions with many festivals. Its theaters offer dramas that have evolved over hundreds of years. The delicate art of flower arranging can be traced back to antiquity. The Imperial Palace stands within locked gates. It is an island of calm in a world hurtling toward the future.

When a subway rumbles out of a Tokyo station during rush hour, an attendant gathers up the shoes. They lie scattered along the platform a sandal here, a battered tennis shoe there. The attendant lines them up to wait for their owners, who will hobble back to claim them as soon as they can. Tokyo's rush-hour crowds are hard to believe. If someone steps on a passenger's foot and a shoe comes off, the passenger cannot bend down to pick it up.

Tokyo is one of the most crowded cities in the world. At home, at work, and on the streets, its people have adapted to living in very close quarters.

HOME SWEET HOME

Long before a new *danchi* (public apartment) is completed in Tokyo, people start buying lottery tickets. The drawing will decide who can move into the brand-new apartments. Demand is so great that the chances of winning an apartment are only 1 in 100.

Since World War II, the population of Tokyo has doubled and redoubled. Each year, hundreds of thousands of people move to the capital in search of jobs. The housing shortage keeps getting worse. Many Tokyo families live in tiny apartments stacked up in high-rise buildings. Others live in traditional neighborhoods. Along winding alleyways stand small wooden houses with fenced yards and gardens of flowers. Tiny shops sell everything from mousetraps to hairdryers. Children play marbles on the sidewalks.

Whether home is an old house or a modern apartment, Tokyo residents leave their shoes at the door. By taking off their shoes, they seem to shed the dirt and confusion of the streets. Home is a place of peace, safe from the noise and pressure outside.

Traditional Japanese dining tables are only a few inches high. Families sit on cushions as they eat their meals.

About 10 million commuters jam Tokyo's trains and subways each day. At the busiest stations, "pushers" shove people into the train cars and force the doors shut. A good pusher can cram 300 people into a car designed for only 100.

In most Tokyo homes, the floors are covered with thick straw mats called *tatami*. Tatami comes in a standard size, about 3 feet by 6 feet. Thus, when someone refers to a "four-mat room" or a "six-mat room," everyone knows how large the space must be.

Traditional Japanese furnishings are low and simple. Tables stand only a few inches high. At meals, everyone sits around the table on cushions instead of chairs. Tokyo apartments have no bedrooms. At bedtime, light mattresses or *futons* are folded down from closets (*oshiire*) in the walls. Few Japanese homes have central heating. In the winter, rooms can grow very cold. Then, the bedding is covered with a nest of futons.

This nursery-school child has been playing on the play-ground, so she washes her feet before going back into the school.

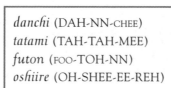

danchi (DAH-NN-CHEE)
tatami (TAH-TAH-MEE)
futon (FOO-TOH-NN)
oshiire (OH-SHEE-EE-REH)

11

These teenagers are getting ready to fly a big kite in one of Tokyo's parks.

On weekends, people flock to Tokyo's parks and playgrounds. Children play baseball and other games, happy to be outdoors. But even the parks are packed with people. One-tenth of the city's land is devoted to recreation. It seems like a lot, but it amounts to only one square yard of land for each man, woman, and child in the city.

Despite the crowding, Tokyo has very little crime. Graffiti is almost unknown. New York City has 150 times more robberies and murders than Tokyo. Many people believe that the Japanese are so law-abiding because of the way they are raised. In Japan, children are taught to be polite and to respect their elders.

One sign of respect in Tokyo is the bow. People bow to one another all day long—students to teachers, workers to employers, hosts

A mother reading a bilingual (Japanese-English) book to her sons

to guests, and guests to hosts. In department stores, young women stand at the escalators, welcoming customers to each floor. Each customer receives a bow and a few courteous words of greeting. On a busy day, one department-store greeter may bow a back-

breaking 65,000 times.

Tokyo is a remarkably modern city. Yet its people still live within religious traditions that date back thousands of years.

The men pictured on pages 12 and 13 are bowing to one another on a Tokyo street corner.

All the Comforts of Home

Many homes in Tokyo's older sections do not have hot running water. Such neighborhoods have *sento* (public bath-houses) for men and women. The public bath is not only a place for getting clean and refreshed. It offers a chance for people to relax and chat, shrouded in clouds of steam. As Tokyo continues to become more modern, however, the bathhouses are start-ing to disappear.

THE LIFE OF THE SPIRIT

Tucked among the skyscrapers of central Tokyo is a stone monument to a nobleman named Taira Masakado. According to legend, Masakado rebelled against the emperor. He was beheaded as punishment. For centuries, a memorial pillar in Tokyo's present-day business district marked the spot where Masakado met his death. During the rebuilding after the 1923 earthquake, the pillar was removed to make room for a new office building. The businessmen who worked there were plagued with bad luck. Some suddenly went bankrupt. Others died in mysterious accidents. Clearly, something was wrong. The businessmen suspected that Masakado's spirit was unhappy. They set up a

This Shinto priest is preparing to bless children at the Meiji Shrine. The paper tree is a symbol for pine branches that are waved during the blessing.

On Adults Day, twenty-year-old women dressed in beautiful kimonos go to the Meiji Shrine to be blessed.

Taira Masakado (TAH-EE-RAH MAH-SAH-KAH-DOH)
Shintô (SHEE-NN-TOH-OH)
Buddhism (BOO-DIH-ZUM)
kami (KAH-MEE)
Meiji (MEH-EE-JEE)

new pillar in his honor, and from then on, they prospered in good health.

Tokyo has two major religions, Shinto and Buddhism. Shinto is an ancient religion that is unique to Japan. Followers of Shinto believe natural objects contain spiritual forces. There are gods of wind, clouds, trees, rocks, and stars. No one can say how many of these gods, or *kami*, exist. They are sometimes referred to as "the eight million."

A Shinto shrine is usually small and modest, nestled within a grove of tall trees. The grounds outside are as important as the building itself. The area is carefully landscaped with gardens and pools, a tribute to the spirits in nature.

This memorial pillar honors Taira Masakado.

This is the entrance to the Meiji Shrine, one of the most sacred Shinto shrines in Japan.

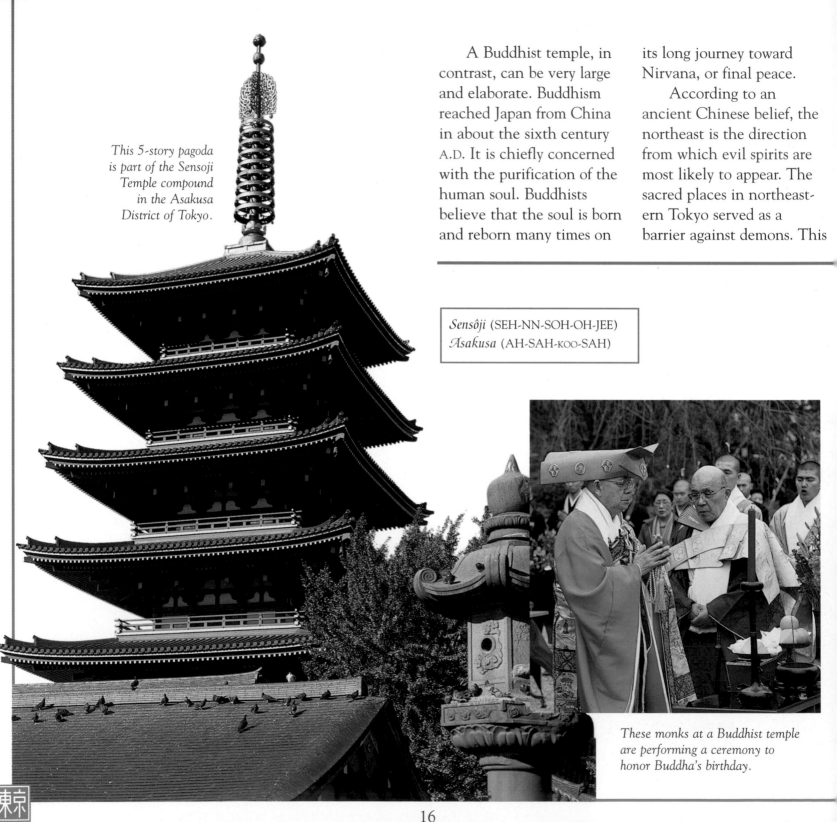

This 5-story pagoda is part of the Sensoji Temple compound in the Asakusa District of Tokyo.

A Buddhist temple, in contrast, can be very large and elaborate. Buddhism reached Japan from China in about the sixth century A.D. It is chiefly concerned with the purification of the human soul. Buddhists believe that the soul is born and reborn many times on its long journey toward Nirvana, or final peace.

According to an ancient Chinese belief, the northeast is the direction from which evil spirits are most likely to appear. The sacred places in northeastern Tokyo served as a barrier against demons. This

Sensôji (SEH-NN-SOH-OH-JEE)
Asakusa (AH-SAH-KOO-SAH)

These monks at a Buddhist temple are performing a ceremony to honor Buddha's birthday.

mystical barrier has been nicknamed the "Incense Screen."

Some people in Tokyo consider themselves Buddhists, and others strictly follow Shinto beliefs. But most Japanese people comfortably embrace both religions. Weddings are usually Shinto ceremonies, celebrating love and the promise of children. On the other hand, Buddhist priests conduct most funerals. It is Buddhism that prepares the soul for the next stage on its long journey.

Most Japanese couples are married in Shinto ceremonies.

Left: A Japanese Buddhist monk at Sensoji Temple

Below: These children are dressed to honor Buddha's birthday.

Fall seven times, but on the eighth get up, runs a Japanese proverb. The people of Tokyo have taken these words to heart. Again and again, their city has been destroyed—by fire, by earthquake, and by war. Yet time after time, it has risen from the ashes. Each time, it has been rebuilt stronger than before.

THE CASTLE ON THE HILL

By the fifteenth century, Japan was a thriving island nation that was protected by the sea from invaders. It was free to develop literature, painting, and sculpture. Culture flourished at the city of Kyoto on the large island of Honshu. East of Kyoto, the land was still wild and rugged. Mounted warriors galloped over the hills. They answered to no law but their own.

In 1457, a warrior chieftain named Ota Dokan built a stone fort on a hill. It overlooked this wild plain. The site was well defended against enemies. It also had a harbor for ships. Over the next century, a settlement grew up around the fort. This outpost on Honshu's eastern shore was known as Edo.

On August 1, 1590, a rising warlord named Tokugawa Ieyasu seized control of Edo. At the site of Ota Dokan's crumbling fort, Ieyasu began work on a splendid castle. The nearest stone quarries were more than 100 miles away. Such details did not halt Ieyasu's ambition. For the next 10 years, ships sailed into Edo Harbor. Each ship bore two huge stones. They were called "hundred-man stones." It took a crew of 100 workmen to move each one. Slowly, year by year, the castle took shape.

Ieyasu went on to design a magnificent city. He filled in parts of Tokyo Bay to create more land. Hibiya, Ginza, and other neighborhoods in the heart of today's Tokyo were originally laid out by Ieyasu and his officials. Kyoto, to the west, remained the political capital of Japan. It was home to the emperor. But the real power lay in Edo, with Ieyasu and his descendants. Under the direction of these warlords, or *shoguns,* Edo became the seat of culture, trade, and power. It surpassed every other city in Japan.

In 1616, the year of Ieyasu's death, an English traveler visited Edo. He marveled at the city's bustling harbor and teeming markets, its shrines, pagodas, and elegant mansions. He was dazzled by Edo Castle. "[It] is a place very strong," he wrote, "double ditched and stone walled about. . . . The [shogun's] palace is a huge thing, all

This bridge in Edo was regarded as the center of the empire.

The feudal lords of Edo traveled around their estates on horseback.

the rooms being gilded with gold, both overhead and upon the walls, except some mixture of paintings amongst of lions, tigers, panthers, eagles, and other beasts and fowls, very lively drawn."

In 1657, fire swept through Edo. The glorious palace was destroyed. This was only the first of many such disasters to strike the city. The shoguns rebuilt the castle. They went on with their plans for the expansion of Edo. By 1700, Edo boasted some 1.3 million people. For several decades, it was the largest city in the world.

Ôta Dôkan (OH-OH-TAH DOH-OH-KAH-NN)
Tokugawa Ieyasu (TOH-KOO-GAH-WAH EE-EH-YOO-su)
Hibiya (HEE-BEE-YAH)
Ginza (GEE-NN-ZAH)
shôgun (SHO-OH-GOO-NN)

MEETING THE WORLD OUTSIDE

In 1715, a Sicilian priest named John Baptiste Sidotti died in Edo's "Christian Prison." Sidotti was the last Christian missionary to work in Japan under the shoguns. He died a martyr's death.

When Tokugawa Ieyasu took over Edo, Christian missionaries were hard at work throughout Japan. Thousands of Japanese people gave up their traditional religions. They adopted the new faith from faraway Europe. The shoguns feared that these converts might not be loyal subjects. In the early 1600s, they persecuted missionaries and their followers. Thousands of people were executed.

The shoguns' distrust of missionaries led to a suspicion of all things foreign. Foreigners were not allowed to visit Japan. Japanese citizens were not allowed to travel abroad. The shoguns were afraid they would be infected with dangerous new ideas. Shipbuilding came to a halt. Anyone caught trying

Above left: A group of Japanese warriors called samurai

Left: Dutch traders warning Ieyasu against the missionaries who were teaching the Japanese people about Christianity

samurai (SAH-MOO-RAH-EE)

Commodore Matthew Perry meeting with the Japanese to make a trade agreement

to leave the country was imprisoned or put to death.

For nearly 200 years, Japan remained isolated from the rest of the world. The United States wanted to open up trade with the mysterious island nation. In 1853, Commodore Matthew Perry sailed into Edo Bay with four powerful warships. By then, the shoguns had grown weak and corrupt. The people of Japan were eager for a change. Commodore Perry opened the country to contact with the world outside.

Many Japanese people began dressing in western clothing after the country was opened to foreign trade.

In the years that followed, the Japanese people embraced everything from the lands across the sea. On the streets of Edo, children bounced balls to a new chant: "Gas lamps, steam engines, horse-carriages, cameras, telegrams, newspapers, schools, post offices, steamboats."

Men and women dressed in clothes from Europe and the United States. It was even suggested that English should replace Japanese as the national language.

In 1868, the last of the Tokugawa shoguns tumbled from power. The emperor took control of the country once more. He shifted his official capital to Edo, and moved into Edo Castle. To show that a brand-new era had begun, Edo received a new name. It was called Tokyo, or "eastern capital."

Japanese emperor Mutsuhito, shown here with his family, took control of the country in 1868. The emperor moved the capital to Edo and changed its name to Tokyo.

Mutsuhito, also known as the Meiji Emperor, moved into what is now called the Imperial Palace (above). The Nijubashi Bridge, shown in the picture, spans a moat on the palace grounds.

Nijubashi (NEE-JOO-BAH-SHEE)

A DEADLY EARTHQUAKE

On September 1, 1923, a violent earthquake buckled the streets of Tokyo. Buildings were wrenched from their foundations. Stoves overturned. Gas mains snapped. Deadly fires flared all over the city. The Kanto Earthquake, as it is known, left vast sections of Tokyo in ruins. No one knows for certain how many people lost their lives. As many as 140,000 were dead or missing. Yet, once again, the people set to work. Within seven years, a new city rose upon the rubble of the old.

Below: Immediately after the 1923 earthquake, workers began removing wreckage from Tokyo streets—even though the ground continued to shake.
Opposite: The ruins of Tokyo after the earthquake (top) and the same scene four years later (bottom)

Human Pillars

When workers were repairing the Imperial Palace after the earthquake of 1923, they found several human skeletons beneath its walls. They were a tragic reminder of the ancient belief that a building must have "human pillars" in its foundation. Palace servants volunteered to sacrifice their lives for the good of the realm. Human bodies were thought to appease evil spirits, insuring that the building would stand firm for generations to come.

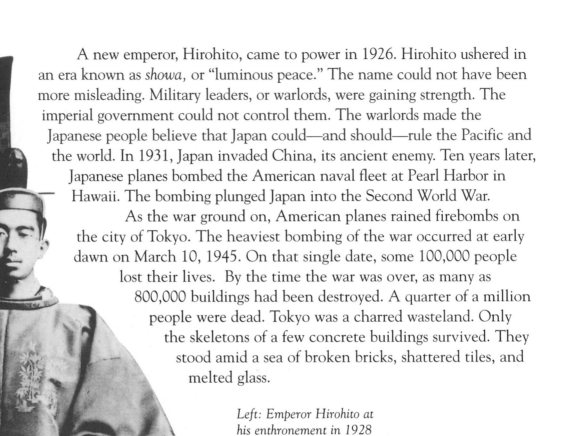

A new emperor, Hirohito, came to power in 1926. Hirohito ushered in an era known as *showa,* or "luminous peace." The name could not have been more misleading. Military leaders, or warlords, were gaining strength. The imperial government could not control them. The warlords made the Japanese people believe that Japan could—and should—rule the Pacific and the world. In 1931, Japan invaded China, its ancient enemy. Ten years later, Japanese planes bombed the American naval fleet at Pearl Harbor in Hawaii. The bombing plunged Japan into the Second World War.

As the war ground on, American planes rained firebombs on the city of Tokyo. The heaviest bombing of the war occurred at early dawn on March 10, 1945. On that single date, some 100,000 people lost their lives. By the time the war was over, as many as 800,000 buildings had been destroyed. A quarter of a million people were dead. Tokyo was a charred wasteland. Only the skeletons of a few concrete buildings survived. They stood amid a sea of broken bricks, shattered tiles, and melted glass.

Left: Emperor Hirohito at his enthronement in 1928

Hirohito (HEE-ROH-HEE-TOH)
shôwa (SHO-OH-WAH)

The people of Tokyo, and of all Japan, found it hard to believe their total defeat. No fire, no earthquake in history had ever brought such utter ruin. Yet, as the proverb told them, they knew they must get up again. They began to clear the rubble from the streets. They hammered together makeshift huts of burnt planks. Soon they could build more substantial homes. They planted gardens in yards thick with ashes. As flowers burst into bloom, Tokyo fought its way back to life.

The Japanese invaded China in 1931 (left) and bombed the American naval fleet at Pearl Harbor in 1941 (below). By the end of World War II, Tokyo was in ashes. Today, the modern city's night sky blazes with neon lights (above).

Today, Tokyo is a modern city. Its streets are canyons between towering walls of glass and steel. At night, its sky blazes with flashing neon lights. Yet, tucked here and there in the highrise wilderness, are relics of the past. Buddhist temples, Shinto shrines, and

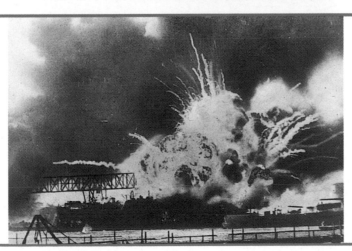

hidden neighborhoods of tiny wooden houses and twisting streets still survive. Despite its trials by fire, Tokyo has not forgotten its traditions. They shape the city today, as they molded it throughout its history.

Japan is a leader in the world's economy. Tokyo is its financial hub. Business leaders in other countries sometimes moan that the Japanese work too hard. It isn't fair, they complain. No one else can hope to compete.

The people of Tokyo do work hard, and students study hard at school. City residents play hard, too. They love festivals and sports, and they enjoy their parks. They hunger for the chance to relax, to put the office and the classroom behind them, to throw themselves into having fun.

HOLIDAY TIME

Shinto and Buddhism provide Tokyo with a year-round calendar of festivals. Many Shinto festivals, or *matsuri*, are held annually. Most matsuri begin with a religious ceremony. The ceremony is followed by processions and dancing. These festivities are meant to please the gods, but they are a delight to mortals as well.

Many matsuri involve rice, Japan's staple food. The Ta-asobi festival is celebrated in early spring. Boys and old men pantomime the planting, tending, and harvesting of the rice crop. When the rice is harvested, everyone dances with joy, to the beat of a great round drum.

Beautifully costumed participants in Tokyo's Oiran-Dochu Parade.

matsuri (MAH-TSOO-REE)
Ta-asobi (TAH-AH-SOH-BEE)

Every April, huge crowds of people celebrate the cherry blossoms at Ueno Park.

The Shinto religion celebrates nature. Flowers are nature at its most beautiful. The people of Tokyo love flowers—planting them, admiring them, arranging them. In parks throughout the city, a series of blossom celebrations are held. The Plum Blossom Festival takes place in February and the Chrysanthemum Festival is held in October. The most spectacular is the Cherry Blossom Festival of early April. People vie for picnic spots under the trees, which shimmer with cherry blooms. Store shelves are crammed with cherry-filled pastries and cherry-flavored candy.

The Chrysanthemum Festival in October is one of many popular flower celebrations in Tokyo.

On January 15, young women in stunning *kimonos* stream into Tokyo's Buddhist temples. The kimono is the traditional costume of Japan. It is a flowing robe bound at the waist with a wide sash called an *obi*. January 15 is Coming of Adult's Day. It is set aside to honor women and men who reached the age of twenty in the preceding year.

Another special day in Tokyo is May 5, Children's Day. A banner shaped like a carp flies over every house where a boy lives. The carp is a very hardy fish that swims upstream against the current each spring. Parents encourage their sons to be as strong and fearless as the carp.

This little girl is taking part in the Seven-Five-Three celebration on November 15.

kimono (KEE-MOH-NOH)
obi (OH-BEE)

These twenty-year-old men are participating in the Adult's Day ceremony at the Meiji Temple.

Boys and girls also celebrate on Seven-Five-Three Day, November 15. On this holiday, seven- and three-year-old girls and five-year-old boys go to the temple. Afterward, there are refreshments for the whole family.

Wind socks shaped like carp fly in the wind on Children's Day, May 5.

This young girl dressed in a beautiful kimono is part of the Seven-Five-Three Festival.

On New Year's Day, a national holiday, huge crowds of people flock to the Meiji Shrine.

Only about 2 percent of all Tokyo residents are Christians. Therefore, Christmas is not a religious holiday. Japan, however, has adopted the western custom of exchanging gifts on December 25. In the weeks before Christmas, stores overflow with enticing new toys.

Wishes for the New Year are written on strips of paper and hung up for the gods to read.

This young woman is dressed in her best kimono to visit the Meiji Shrine during New Year's Festival week.

On New Year's Day, Tokyo clamors with temple bells. Starting at 12:00 A.M., in every Buddhist temple across the city, the bells ring out 108 times. Each stroke stands for one of the 108 human passions that the soul must overcome on its journey to Nirvana. The bells signal the end of the old year and the start of the new, a time of rebirth. New Year's Day is a national holiday. People flock to temples and shrines. Following an ancient tradition, some people write wishes on strips of paper. They hang them up for the gods to read. Whether they follow this custom or not, the people of Tokyo see the beginning of a new year as a time of hope, when all good things are possible.

THE THRILL OF SPORTS

Ryôgoku Kokugikan
(LYOH-OH-GOH-koo
KOH-KOO-GHEE-KAH-NN)
yokozuna (YOH-KOH-DZOO-
NAH)

When a pair of sumo wrestlers meet in the ring, the impact resounds through the stands. The contest between these massive men is like the collision of two mountains. Sumo wrestling is Japan's national sport. Three of the major tournaments are held each year at Ryogoku Kokugikan Tournament Hall in eastern Tokyo.

Sumo wrestlers begin to train when they are in their early teens. They must be powerful and enormous. They weigh from 300 to 400 pounds. The tournaments each year determine who will become the new *yokozuna*, or grand champion. Because they are such large men, sumo wrestlers have huge appetites. Prizes at tournaments may include large supplies of beef, mushrooms, and rice.

In Tokyo's middle schools, some children begin to learn *kendo*, or "the way of the sword." Kendo is a form of fencing that dates back to the shogun era. Warriors, or samurai, used special two-handed swords in battle. Today, kendo is taught as a form of physical and mental exercise.

Sumo wrestlers, like these two, weigh from 200 to 300 pounds.

kendô (KEH-NN-DOH-OH)

38

A kendo pose with the weapon in a raised position

In addition to kendo, the Japanese practice many other martial arts whose roots are buried in history. *Jujitsu*, *karate*, and *aikido* developed as fighting methods based on the philosophy of Buddhism. In jujitsu and its more modern form, *judo*, the fighter uses the opponent's strength and weight to throw him or her off balance. Karate depends on kicking and striking the opponent with the hands, elbows, and knees. Aikido is a self-defense system based on immobilizing holds and twisting throws. Many Japanese study the martial arts, and go to special halls to watch the professionals perform.

As deeply as they honor their own traditions, the Japanese also love all things American. No game is more American than baseball. The Japanese began playing baseball in 1873. Today, Tokyo has four teams that play in the Japanese major leagues. The most popular are the Tokyo Giants, who play at Tokyo Dome. Unlike American baseball players, Japanese players practice year-round. In Tokyo, people work hard, even when it comes to games.

jûjitsu (JOO-OO-JEE-TSOO)
karate (KAH-RAH-TEH)
aikidô (AH-EE-KEE-DOH-OH)
jûdô (JOO-OO-DOH-OH)

These Little League baseball players are waiting their turn to play their game for the championship. Ball games are played throughout the day until one team wins the season tournament.

THE PLAY'S THE THING

In Tokyo's Koubo District stands a round, pink building with twin gables and a cupola on its roof. It is patterned after London's famous Globe Theater. That was where Shakespeare's plays were first performed 400 years ago. Since 1988, Tokyo's version of the Globe has offered a wide variety of foreign plays. They range from Shakespearean tragedies to comedies by Neil Simon. Plays are performed in Japanese or in their original languages.

Tokyo has its own rich theatrical traditions as well. The ancient *noh* theater is more like dance than drama. Movements are slow and stately, and the lines are chanted. From time to time, the audience is treated to brief comic interludes called *kyogen*. In the kyogen, actors perform short, humorous folktales. This provides a refreshing break from the serious drama of the noh play.

The best-known form of Japanese theater is *kabuki*. The word kabuki means "song-dance-skill." Kabuki theater involves both singing and dancing. Its actors are highly trained. In all performances, the cast is entirely male. Men take even the female parts. The stage is sometimes crowded with musicians,

---

Koubo (KOH-OO-BOH) *kyôgen* (KYOH-OH-GHEH-NN) *fugu* (FOO-GOO)
nôh (NOH-OH) *kabuki* (KAH-BOO-kee)

Good Enough to Eat

A favorite Tokyo pastime is dining out. Restaurant windows display realistic plastic models of the food to be enjoyed within. This might include grilled eels, deep-fried vegetables in batter, and a luscious assortment of noodle dishes. One rare delicacy is *fugu*, a type of blowfish that is poisonous if it is not properly cooked.

40

Kabuki actors, like those shown on this page, wear magnificent costumes and are skilled in both singing and dancing.

bunraku (BOO-NN-RAH-koo)

narrators, and sound-effects men with gongs and wooden clappers. The actors wear magnificent costumes. A kabuki play usually lasts four or five hours. There are two or three breaks for tea and meals. Some members of the audience drift in and out.

One of the most fascinating forms of theater to be seen in Tokyo is *bunraku*. In bunraku, the drama is enacted by large, elaborate puppets. Each is operated by a team of three puppeteers. The puppets are made with careful detail. They can move their fingers, open their eyes, write letters, and imitate eating with chopsticks. The puppeteers are all perfectly visible, and their maneuvers are part of the fun.

Tokyo has been rebuilt twice in the twentieth century. It was reconstructed after the 1923 Kanto Earthquake, and again after the bombing of World War II. It bears all the marks of a new city, its face turned boldly toward the future. Yet Japanese society is deeply rooted in tradition. Tokyo cherishes many relics of its long history. Its temples and shrines, gardens and neighborhoods preserve a rich and undying heritage.

REACHING FOR THE SKY

The year 1936 saw the completion of the Tokyo Tower. It looks very much like the Eiffel Tower in Paris. The tower climbs an astonishing 1,192 feet into the sky. It is the tallest structure in all of Tokyo. It is especially remarkable because the city is so prone to earthquakes. The foundations go very deep to help it withstand a major tremor.

From the observation deck at the tower's crown, Tokyo seems to sprawl without pattern or reason. Its streets weave between highrises. Clusters of low wooden houses are nearly hidden by lofty office buildings and department stores. A tangle of highways cuts the city into oddly shaped scraps.

The Tokyo Tower, completed in 1936, looks very much like the Eiffel Tower in Paris.

A sunset aerial view of Tokyo's Asakusa District

This policewoman works in the Ginza section of Tokyo.

When Tokyo natives describe the location of a city landmark, they say that it is "just north of the Imperial Palace," or "southwest of the palace about two kilometers."

The Imperial Palace is Tokyo's center. Not far to the south stands the National Diet Building. This is Japan's legislature, much like Congress in the United States.

East of the Imperial Palace is the Marunouchi District. It is a forest of modern office buildings. The Ginza is south of Marunouchi. It is Tokyo's most elegant shopping section. The Ginza sparkles with fashionable clothing stores. Other shops specialize in electronics, pearls, pianos, or motorcycles. Loudspeakers blare commercial messages onto the sidewalks: "See our new leather handbags! Just what you've been looking for!" At the Ginza's main intersection stands a stone lion. It is a replica of the famous statue in London's Trafalgar Square. Friends often arrange to meet at the lion for a day of shopping and fun.

Marunouchi
(MAH-ROO-NOH-OO-CHEE)

A busy day in Tokyo's Ginza District

Shoppers, tourists, and
families on an outing enjoy
the chance to participate in
the Ginza experience.

春陽文庫

1995

...り 酒
...全集 4 ——

新・茶捕物帳—三日月に哭く

...沢左保

角川文庫

Kanda (KAH-NN-DAH)
Asakusa (AH-SAH-ĸoo-SAH)

Northeast of the Imperial Palace is the Kanda. This is a quiet section with hundreds of bookstores. Tokyo natives love to read, and shops in the Kanda are an open invitation. Beyond the Kanda is the Asakusa District, Tokyo's leading entertainment section. The Asakusa is alive with restaurants, movie theaters, and amusement parks. The Temple of Kannon in the Asakusa honors the Buddhist goddess of mercy. It is a welcome retreat from the city's noise and excitement.

These uniformed children are enjoying a field trip to the Shinjuku section of Tokyo.

Shinjuku Station is the most heavily traveled stop along Tokyo's crowded railway system. It serves the Shinjuku section, a vast subcity west of the Imperial Palace. The east side of Shinjuku is the older part of the area. Here there are large department stores, small shops, movie theaters, bars, and restaurants. An underground shopping arcade extends for nearly a mile along gleaming tiled corridors. West of the railroad station, Shinjuku bursts into the modern world of highrise office buildings and apartments. The centerpiece of this bustling section is a 144-acre park, the Shinjuku Gyoen. As the seasons turn, the park has one glorious offering after another—cherry blossoms in April, irises in June, chrysanthemums in the fall.

Shinjuku Gyôen (SHEE-NN-JOO-KOO GHOH-OH-EH-NN)

When spring comes, these snow-covered trees in Shinjuku Gyoen will be covered with blossoms.

FROM THE CENTER OUTWARD

Ueno, on Tokyo's northeastern edge, has been a center of culture and study since the eighteenth century. It is the home of several colleges and universities, as well as many of Tokyo's finest museums. Crowds flock to the National Tokyo Museum for exhibits of ancient Buddhist sculpture, sixteenth-century brush painting, or modern abstract creations. The National Museum of Western Art displays priceless works by such masters as Van Gogh, Matisse, and Monet.

The National Museum of Western Art in Ueno Park draws large crowds of visitors.

Ueno (OO-EH-NOH)

Ueno Park is the oldest public park in all of Tokyo. Hikers explore trails among the trees, and ducks paddle on placid ponds. One of the park's treasures is a 5-tiered wooden pagoda. It was built in 1639 and dedicated to the Tokugawa shoguns. Constructed of many small, interlocking panels of wood, the pagoda has unusual flexibility. This quality has enabled it to survive many earthquakes. Today, engineers are seeking ways to use this design as they construct new earthquake-proof buildings.

This 5-tiered wooden pagoda in Ueno Park was built in 1639.

Young couples and families like to go boating on Shinobazu Pond in Ueno Park. Children love the colorful balloons that are sold in the park.

Tokyo still has many charming traditional neighborhoods, each with its shrines and temples. One good example is Rokubancho. It is hard to drive on the narrow, twisting streets. It's easier to walk. Most of the houses are small and neat. Each has a lovingly tended garden. Here and there, a more stately residence stands behind locked gates. The tall trees leaning over the walls hint at the splendor within.

Tokyo's face is constantly changing. About one-fourth of all the jobs in Japan are based in the capital city. Despite the overcrowding, people stream in from town and countryside looking for work. As Tokyo's population swells, developers search greedily for more land. Year by year, rice fields around the outskirts are gobbled up by the public apartments called danchi. In many places, bulldozers have leveled hills to make more room for new apartment complexes.

Rokubanchô (ROH-KOO-BAH-NN-CHOH-OH)

These buildings are among Tokyo's many danchi, or public apartments.

52

Because Tokyo is such a crowded city, housing is very expensive and hard to find. Most families live in tiny apartments or houses that are very close to one another.

ku (KOO)
chôme (CHOH-OH-MEH)

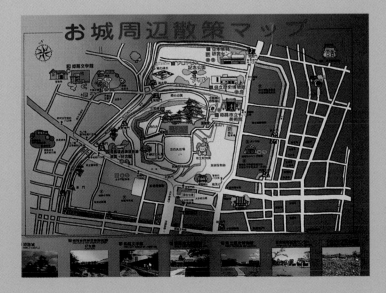

Lost and Found

For a visitor, locating a friend's house in Tokyo can be a major challenge. Only the main streets have names. Furthermore, houses are not numbered consecutively, but according to when they were built. Instead of a street and house number, a Tokyo address includes the district, or *ku*; the neighborhood; and the section, or *chome*, where the house stands. A chome is generally about the size of one or two square city blocks. Within some chomes, maps are displayed at street corners, showing each house with the family's name.

Hachijô (HAH-CHEE-JOH-OH)

*Fishing is the main occupation
on Hachijo Island. This
woman is mending a fishing net.*

One corner of Tokyo
seems almost untouched by
the modern world. Hachijo
Island lies 170 miles off in
Tokyo Bay. Officially, it is
part of the city proper.
About 13,000 people live
on Hachijo, with its
windswept hills and beaches
of black lava. Fishing is the
chief occupation among the
islanders. With Hachijo,
Tokyo has the widest city
limits in the world.

An aerial view of Hachijo Island

Hachijo seems a world away from bustling downtown Tokyo. But even amid the highrises, Tokyo has an island of peace. It is the Imperial Palace. Twice a year, on New Year's Day and on the emperor's birthday, the citizens of Japan are invited in for a visit. On those special occasions, people by the thousands cross the famous Nijubashi Bridge. This spans one of the palace's inner moats. Packed tightly together, the visitors listen in silent reverence to the emperor's words of greeting. They are awed in this sacred place, the vital heart of their capital city, Tokyo.

The Imperial Palace is an island of peace in the heart of Tokyo.

FAMOUS LANDMARKS

Mount Fuji

Tokyo Tower

Ueno Park

Mount Fuji
Some 70 miles west of Tokyo, this snowcapped volcano could once be viewed from most parts of Tokyo. With modern pollution, it is now visible only about one day out of every seven.

Imperial Palace
Home of Japan's emperor and his family. The extensive grounds contain woodlands, ponds, and gardens. The imperial residence itself is a modern building completed in 1970.

Tokyo Tower
Radio and television broadcasting tower in downtown Tokyo. Standing 1,192 feet tall, the Tokyo Tower may be the highest man-made structure on earth.

Ueno Park
Tokyo's largest park, covering 210 acres. The park contains the Tokyo National Museum, the Museum of Western Art, the National Museum of Science, and the Ueno Zoo.

The Meiji Shrine
Shinto shrine in the Yoyogi District of western Tokyo. The shrine is dedicated to the "Meiji Emperor," who moved the capital to Tokyo in 1868. His wife, the Dowager Empress Shoken, is also honored.

Sensoji Temple
Buddhist temple dedicated to Kannon, goddess of mercy. According to legend, the temple was built after three fishermen found a golden statue of the goddess in their net. The statue is still housed in the temple, though it is not shown to the public.

Yasukuni Shrine
Shinto shrine dedicated to Japan's war dead. Traditional festivals are held here in April and October.

Korakuen Garden and Rikugien Garden
Two famous gardens located north of the Imperial Palace. Noted for their beautifully landscaped grounds, they are among the oldest gardens in the city. Charming teahouses are scattered along the meandering pathways.

The Museum of Western Art in Ueno Park

Sensoji Temple and Pagoda

National Diet Building
The home of Japan's lawmaking body, or Diet. It is a structure of concrete and granite with a distinctive central tower. The Diet is located southwest of the Imperial Palace.

Akasaka Palace
Japan's official state guest house. It was originally the home of the Crown Prince. From the outside, the building resembles Britain's Buckingham Palace.

National Stadium
The largest sports stadium in Japan. Located in Meiji Park, it was the main site of the 1964 Olympic Games.

Hibiya Park
An oasis of green and quiet in Tokyo's bustling business district. Crowds gather to enjoy the new blossoms that appear as the seasons change from spring to summer to autumn.

Sengakuji Temple
This temple is famous throughout Japan as the place where 47 samurai warriors once avenged the death of their master and then committed mass suicide. Their remains are buried on the temple grounds.

The Ginza
Tokyo's glittering shopping strip. A key landmark is the statue of a lion at the entrance to the Mitsukoshi Department Store. Friends often arrange to meet there.

Kasumigaseki Building
A 36-story office building, completed in 1968. It offers an excellent view into the walled Imperial Palace grounds. Tokyo residents often use this building as a measure of great volume. Someone might say, for example, "I'm hungry enough to eat a Kasumigaseki of rice!"

Nihombashi Bridge
Bridge noted for its European Renaissance style. To the people of Tokyo, it is a symbolic link with the rest of Japan, the beginning of roads into the world beyond the capital.

FAST FACTS

POPULATION 1997

Tokyo:	7,830,323
Metropolitan area:	11,680,490

Tokyo is the fourth largest city in the world. Only Mexico City (Mexico), Seoul (South Korea), and Moscow (Russia) have more people.

AREA 223 square miles

CLIMATE Tokyo is in the temperate zone, with warm summers and cold winters. The average temperature in January is 39 degrees Fahrenheit. In July, the average temperature is 76 degrees Fahrenheit. Annual precipitation (rain and snowfall) averages 58 inches.

GOVERNMENT Tokyo's chief executive, or governor, is elected to a 4-year term.

ECONOMY Tokyo is the center of Japan's thriving economy. About 25 percent of the jobs in Japan are based in Tokyo. Tokyo is a world leader in the manufacture of electrical products including televisions, radios, cassette recorders, and computer equipment. Publishing is also a major industry. Tokyo produces 25 daily newspapers, as well as thousands of books and pamphlets each year. Other manufactured goods include processed foods, chemicals, furniture, and paper. Tokyo is also a center of banking and finance. The Tokyo Stock Exchange handles shares from more than 1,300 companies, more than are traded on the stock exchange in New York.

TRANSPORTATION Though Tokyo has an extensive network of modern freeways, its roads cannot handle the heavy automobile traffic. The city is frequently snarled with traffic jams.

CHRONOLOGY

1457
Ota Dokan builds a fort on a hill near Tokyo Bay

1590
Tokugawa Ieyasu begins work on Edo Castle

1603
Ieyasu establishes himself as military leader, or shogun, and founds the Tokugawa shogunate

1627
Kaneiji Temple is built on Ueno Hill to protect the city from the evil spirits that dwell to the northeast

1657
Much of Edo is destroyed by fire

1660
Construction of Edo's first kabuki theater, the Kabuki-Za

1700
With 1.3 million people, Edo is the largest city in the world

1707
Mount Fuji erupts, and Edo is covered with ashes

1853
Commodore Matthew Perry sails into Tokyo Bay and opens Japan to the world outside

1868
The emperor moves from Kyoto to Edo; Edo is renamed Tokyo, meaning "eastern capital"

1923
The Kanto Earthquake strikes Tokyo, destroying much of the city

1926
Emperor Hirohito ushers in the Showa Era, or "Era of Luminous Peace"

Schoolboys visiting a shrine

1931
Japan invades Manchuria, a province in northeastern China

1936
Tokyo Tower, the tallest structure in the city at 1,192 feet, is completed

1941
Japanese planes bomb the American naval fleet at Pearl Harbor in Hawaii; Japan enters World War II

1945
American planes pound Tokyo with nearly 3 million incendiary bombs; most of the city is destroyed

1964
Tokyo hosts the Olympic Games

1970
Work is completed on the new Imperial Palace

1985
The Diet passes an Equal Rights Opportunity Act, improving women's opportunities in employment

1989
Hirohito dies after 62 years as emperor; he is succeeded by his son, Crown Prince Akihito

1992
The Metropolitan Tower is completed. Standing 796 feet tall (50 stories), it is Tokyo's highest office building

1995
Many commuters are injured and several killed when terrorists unleash poison gas in the Tokyo subway

TOKYO

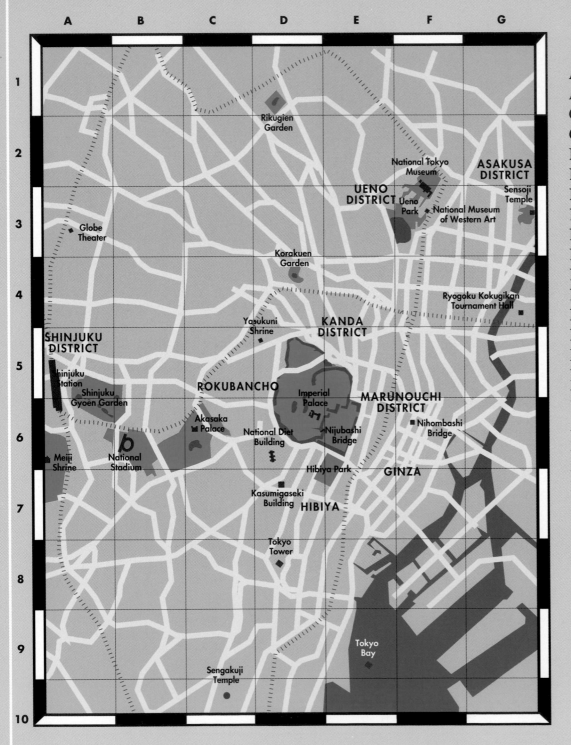

A B C D E F G

1
2
3
4
5
6
7
8
9
10

Rikugien Garden

National Tokyo Museum

UENO DISTRICT
Ueno Park

National Museum of Western Art

ASAKUSA DISTRICT

Sensoji Temple

Globe Theater

Korakuen Garden

Ryogoku Kokugikan Tournament Hall

Yasukuni Shrine

KANDA DISTRICT

SHINJUKU DISTRICT

Shinjuku Station

Shinjuku Gyoen Garden

ROKUBANCHO

Imperial Palace

MARUNOUCHI DISTRICT

Nihombashi Bridge

Akasaka Palace

National Diet Building

Nijubashi Bridge

Meiji Shrine

National Stadium

Kasumigaseki Building

Hibiya Park

HIBIYA

GINZA

Tokyo Tower

Tokyo Bay

Sengakuji Temple

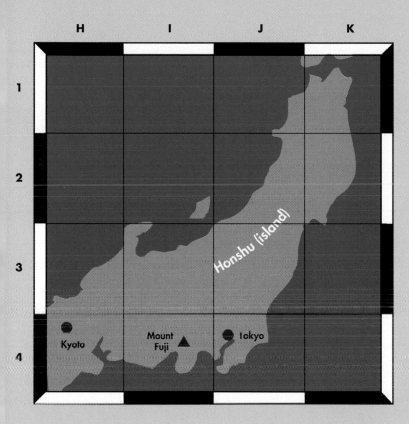

Tokyo Bay	E,F 9, 10
Tokyo Tower	D8
Ueno (district)	E,F 2,3
Ueno Park	E,F 2,3
Yasukuni Shrine	D5

GLOSSARY

Buddhism: Asian religion based on the belief that the soul is reborn many times on its quest for final peace

convert: A person whose belief has changed from one religion to another

flexibility: Ability to yield under pressure

interlude: Break or pause

kimono: The traditional costume of Japan, a graceful robe belted at the waist

legislature: Lawmaking body within a government

martial: Having to do with fighting

martyr: A person who is punished or is put to death because of his or her religious beliefs

missionary: A person who is sent to a region to convert others to a certain religion

moat: Deep ditch designed to keep enemies from invading a castle

oasis: Green, watered area in a desert; place of peace and refreshment

pagoda: Traditional Asian tower; the roof has upturned corners

refuge: Safe haven

replica: Copy

Shinto: A religion native to Japan, based on the belief that all natural objects have spiritual properties

shrine: Sacred place dedicated to a god or saint

technological: Having to do with technology, the science of mechanical and industrial arts

warlord: Military dictator

Picture Identifications

Cover: Fan, the Imperial Palace, young woman in kimono during New Year's Festival week
Page 3: A little girl at the Meiji Shrine on Seven-Five-Three Day
Pages 4-5: The Imperial Palace
Pages 8-9: A crowd of people at a Tokyo festival
Page 18: *Reign of the Shoguns*, seventeenth century
Page 19: Daigo II, an early emperor of Japan
Pages 30-31: Children beating drums during a New Year's celebration
Pages 42-43: Shinjuku Gyoen, a park in the Shinjuku section of Tokyo

Photo Credits:

Cover (top left), ©**KK&A, Ltd**; cover (background), ©Camerique/**H. Armstrong Roberts**; cover (right), ©**Cameramann International, Ltd.**; 1, ©Steve Vidler/**SuperStock International, Inc.**; 3, ©**KK&A, Ltd.**; 4-5, ©Steve Vidlerl/**SuperStock International, Inc.**; 6 (left), ©**Cameramann International, Ltd.**; 6 (flowers), ©**KK&A, Ltd.**; 7 (left), ©Mick Roessler/**SuperStock International, Inc.**; 7 (right), ©Deborah L. Martin/**Unicorn Stock Photos**; 8-9, ©Orion/**Photri, Inc.**; 10 (top), ©Charles Gupton/**Tony Stone Images, Inc.**; 10 (sandals), ©**KK&A, Ltd.**; 11 (top), ©Ron Dahlquist/**SuperStock International, Inc.**; 11 (child's shoes), ©**KK&A, Ltd.**; 11 (bottom right), ©**Cameramann International, Ltd.**; 12 (left), ©Andy Sacks/**Tony Stone Images, Inc.**; 12 (right), ©**Cameramann International, Ltd.**; 13 (left), ©Joel Dexter/**Unicorn Stock Photos**; 13 (right), ©Andy Sacks/**Tony Stone Images, Inc.**; 14 (left), ©Steve Vidler/**SuperStock International, Inc.**; 14 (right), ©**Cameramann International, Ltd.**; 15 (top), ©Orion/**Photri, Inc.**; 15 (bottom), ©Steve Vidler/**SuperStock International, Inc.**; 16 (left), ©Steve Vidler/**SuperStock International, Inc.**; 16 (right), ©**Cameramann International, Ltd.**; 17 (top), ©Noriyuku Yoshida/**SuperStock International, Inc.**; 17 (bottom left), ©Eddie Stangler/**SuperStock International, Inc.**; 17 (bottom right), ©**Cameramann International, Ltd.**; 18 & 19, **Stock Montage, Inc.**; 20 (brush/palette), ©**KK&A, Ltd.**; 21 (left), **The Bettmann Archive**; 21 (right), **Stock Montage, Inc.**; 22 (both pictures), **Stock Montage, Inc.**; 23, **The Bettmann Archive, Inc.**; 24, **Stock Montage, Inc.**; 25 (top), ©Ron Dahlquist/**SuperStock International, Inc.**; 25 (bottom), **The Bettmann Archive**; 26, **UPI/Bettmann**; 27, ©**Archive Photos/Hirz**; 28, ©**Kyodo News**; 29 (top), ©Roy King/**SuperStock International, Inc.**; 29 (middle and bottom), **UPI/Bettmann**; 30-31, ©**Cameramann International, Ltd.**; 32 (chopsticks), ©**KK&A, Ltd.**; 32 (right), ©Steve Vidler/**SuperStock International, Inc.**; 33 (candy), ©**KK&A, Ltd.**; 33 (top right), ©Ron Dahlquist/**SuperStock International, Inc.**; 33 (bottom), ©Orion/**Photri, Inc.**; 34 (left), ©Eddie Stangler/**SuperStock International, Inc.**; 34 (carp), ©**KK&A, Ltd.**; 34 (bottom right), ©**Cameramann International, Ltd.**; 35 (left), ©**Cameramann International, Ltd.**; 35 (right), ©**Photo Edit**; 36, ©Orion/**Photri, Inc.**; 37 (left), ©Orion/**Photri, Inc.**; 37 (right), ©**Cameramann International, Ltd.**; 38, ©Roy Garner/**Rex Features, London**; 39 (top), ©Roderick Chen/**SuperStock International, Inc.**; 39 (bottom), ©**Cameramann International, Ltd.**; 40 (fan), ©**KK&A, Ltd.**; 40 (bottom), ©Paul A. Hein/**Unicorn Stock Photos**; 41 (left), ©**Rex Features, London**; 41 (right), ©Ron Jaffe/**Unicorn Stock Photos**; 42-43, ©Orion/**Photri, Inc.**; 44, ©Ron Dahlquist/**SuperStock International, Inc.**; 45 (left), ©James A. Smestad/**mga/Photri**; 45 (right), ©Orion/**Photri**; 46 (pearls), ©**KK&A, Ltd.**; 46 (bottom), ©**Tony Stone Images, Inc.**; 47 (left), ©Orion/**Photri, Inc.**; 47 (right), ©**H. Armstrong Roberts**; 48 (book and book jacket), ©**KK&A, Ltd.**; 49 (top), ©Ron Dahlquist/**SuperStock International, Inc.**; 49 (bottom), ©Orion/**Photri, Inc.**; 50, ©Orion/**Photri, Inc.**; 51 (top), ©Orion/**Photri, Inc.**; 51 (both bottom pictures), ©**Cameramann International, Ltd.**; 52, ©Orion/**Photri, Inc.**; 53 (top), ©R. Kord/**H. Armstrong Roberts**; 53 (middle), ©Charles Gupton/**Tony Stone Images, Inc.**; 53 (bottom), ©Jean Higgins/**Unicorn Stock Photos**; 54 (top), ©Steve Vidler/**SuperStock International, Inc.**; 54 (bottom), ©Orion/**Photri, Inc.**; 55, ©Orion/**Photri, Inc.**; 56 (left), ©Pascal Crapet/**Tony Stone Images, Inc.**; 56 (middle), ©**H. Armstrong Roberts**; 56 (right), ©**Cameramann International, Ltd.**; 57 (left), ©**Cameramann International, Ltd.**; 57 (right), ©Orion/**Photri, Inc.**; 59, ©George Hunter/**H. Armstrong Roberts**; 60 & 61, ©**KK&A, Ltd.**

INDEX

Page numbers in boldface type indicate illustrations

ABOUT THE AUTHOR

Deborah Kent grew up in Little Falls, New Jersey, and received her B.A. in English from Oberlin College. She earned an M.A. in Social Work from the Smith College of Social Work, and worked for several years at the University Settlement House in New York City. For five years she lived in San Miguel de Allende, Mexico, where she wrote her first novel for young adults. Deborah Kent is the author of a dozen young-adult novels as well as many titles in the Children's Press America the Beautiful series. She lives in Chicago with her husband and their daughter Janna.